What Happens at a Supermarket?/
¿Qué pasa en un supermercado?

By Amy Hutchings

Reading Consultant: Susan Nations, M.Ed.,
author/literacy coach/consultant in literacy development

WEEKLY READER®
PUBLISHING

For a complete list of Where People Work titles,
please visit our web site at **www.garethstevens.com**.
For a free catalog describing Gareth Stevens Publishing's list of high-quality books,
call 1-800-542-2595 (USA) or 1-800-387-3178 (Canada). Our fax: 877-542-2596

Library of Congress Cataloging-in-Publication Data

Hutchings, Amy.
      [What happens at a supermarket? Spanish & English]
      What happens at a supermarket? / by Amy Hutchings; reading consultant,
      Susan Nations / ¿Qué pasa en un supermercado? / por Amy Hutchings;
      consultora de lectura, Susan Nations.
            p. cm. — (Where people work)
      Includes bibliographical references and index.
      ISBN-10: 1-4339-0077-7   ISBN-13: 978-1-4339-0077-8 (lib. bdg.)
      ISBN-10: 1-4339-0141-2   ISBN-13: 978-1-4339-0141-6 (softcover)
      1. Supermarkets—Juvenile literature. I. Nations, Susan. II. Title. III. Title:
      ¿Qué pasa en un supermercado?
  HF5469.H8818   2009
  381'.456413—dc22   2008039349

This edition first published in 2009 by
Weekly Reader® Books
An Imprint of Gareth Stevens Publishing
1 Reader's Digest Road
Pleasantville, NY 10570-7000 USA

Copyright © 2009 by Gareth Stevens, Inc.

Buddy® is a registered trademark of Weekly Reader Corporation. Used under license.

Executive Managing Editor: Lisa M. Herrington
Creative Director: Lisa Donovan
Designers: Michelle Castro, Alexandria Davis
Photographer: Richard Hutchings
Publisher: Keith Garton
Translation: Tatiana Acosta and Guillermo Gutiérrez

Special thanks to the Stop & Shop Supermarket Company and to store managers Bob Silver
and Gary DaVita.

Printed in the United States of America

1 2 3 4 5 6 7 8 9 10 09 08

Hi, Kids!

I'm Buddy, your Weekly Reader® pal. Have you ever been to a supermarket? I'm here to show and tell what happens at a supermarket. So, come on. Turn the page and read along!

- - - - - - - - - -

¡Hola, chicos!

Soy Buddy, su amigo de Weekly Reader®. ¿Han ido alguna vez a un supermercado? Estoy aquí para contarles lo que pasa en un supermercado. Así que vengan conmigo. ¡Pasen la página y vamos a leer!

Boldface words appear in the glossary.

- - - - - - -

Las palabras en **negrita** aparecen en el glosario.

Welcome to the **supermarket**! A supermarket is a store where people buy food and other items.

‒ ‒ ‒ ‒ ‒ ‒ ‒ ‒ ‒

¡Bienvenidos al **supermercado**! Un supermercado es una tienda donde la gente compra alimentos y otros artículos.

Big trucks bring food to the supermarket. Workers unload boxes of food from the trucks.

- - - - - - - - - -

Grandes camiones llevan los alimentos al supermercado. Unos trabajadores descargan las cajas de comida de los camiones.

Workers put out fresh fruits and vegetables. Yum! Look at all the bright yellow bananas.

- - - - - - - -

En la sección de frutas y verduras, los trabajadores exponen esos alimentos. ¡Qué rico! Miren todas esas bananas amarillitas.

Some workers stock the shelves with food. They make sure that shoppers can find what they need.

- - - - - - - - -

Otros trabajadores ponen alimentos en las estanterías. Se aseguran de que los clientes pueden encontrar todo lo que necesitan.

11

The supermarket also has a bakery.
The **baker** makes fresh bread and rolls.
She frosts a birthday cake.

- - - - - - - - - -

En el supermercado también hay una
panadería. La **panadera** hornea panes
y panecillos. También decora las tartas.

baker/
panadera

13

In the **deli**, busy workers slice fresh meat and cheese for sandwiches. They are very careful with the slicing machines.

— — — — — — — — —

En la sección de *deli*, atareados trabajadores cortan embutidos y quesos para los sándwiches. Tienen mucho cuidado cuando usan las rebanadoras.

deli/
deli

15

Behind the scenes, a worker puts out new cartons of milk. He makes sure that milk and other **dairy** foods are fresh.

– – – – – – – – –

Detrás de las neveras, un trabajador repone las botellas de leche. Se asegura de que la leche y los demás productos **lácteos** estén en buen estado.

When shoppers are done, they go to the checkout line. They pay the **cashier** for their groceries.

- - - - - - - - -

Cuando terminan de comprar, los clientes hacen cola en las cajas. Allí, le pagan los productos a la **cajera**.

cashier/
cajera

A bagger puts groceries into cloth bags. The bags can be used for the next visit to the supermarket.

— — — — — — — — —

Un trabajador pone la compra en bolsas de tela. Estas bolsas se pueden usar en la próxima visita al supermercado.

bagger/
trabajador que
embolsa

21

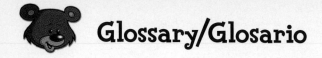

Glossary/Glosario

baker: a person who makes baked goods, such as bread, rolls, cookies, and cakes

cashier: a person who takes in and pays out money in a store

dairy: milk and milk products, such as cheese, butter, and yogurt

deli: a place where ready-to-eat foods such as meat, cheese, and prepared salads are sold

supermarket: a store where people buy groceries

— — — — — — — — —

cajero: persona que recibe dinero y da cambio en una tienda

deli: lugar donde se venden comidas preparadas, embutidos, quesos y ensaladas

lácteos: leche y productos derivados de la leche, como el queso, la mantequilla y el yogurt

panadero: persona que hace y hornea panes, panecillos, galletas y tartas

supermercado: tienda donde la gente compra alimentos

For More Information/Más información

Books/Libros

Grocery Store. Field Trip (series). Angela Leeper (Heinemann, 2004)

My Food Pyramid. (DK Publishing, 2007)

Supermarket. Kathleen Krull (Holiday House, 2001)

Web Site/Página web
PBS Kids: Supermarket Adventure/
PBS Kids: Aventura en el supermercado
www.pbskids.org/arthur/games/supermarket
Go grocery shopping with this exciting supermarket game!/
¡Vayan de compras con este emocionante juego sobre el supermercado!

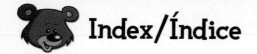# Index/Índice

About the Author

Amy Hutchings was part of the original production staff of *Sesame Street* for the first ten years of the show's history. She then went on to work with her husband, Richard, producing thousands of photographs for children's publishers. She has written several books, including *Firehouse Dog* and *Picking Apples and Pumpkins*. She lives in Rhinebeck, New York, along with many deer, squirrels, and wild turkeys.

Información sobre la autora

Amy Hutchings formó parte del grupo de producción original de la serie *Plaza Sésamo* durante los primeros diez años del programa. Más adelante, pasó a trabajar con su esposo, Richard, en la producción de miles de fotografías para editoriales de libros infantiles. Amy ha escrito muchos libros, incluyendo *Firehouse Dog* y *Picking Apples and Pumpkins*. Vive en Rhinebeck, Nueva York, junto con muchos venados, ardillas y pavos salvajes.